MARIE CURIE

IZZI HOWELL

All inquiries should be addressed to:
Peterson's Publishing, LLC
4380 S. Syracuse Street, Suite 200
Denver, CO 80237-2624
www.petersonsbooks.com

ISBN: 978-1-4380-8933-1

Printed in China

Picture acknowledgements:
Alamy: Lebrecht Music & Arts 6 and 23, Impress 8, Pictorial Press Ltd 11, Lordprice Collection 14, Chronicle 18, Granger Historical Picture Archive 20; Getty: Popperfoto 7, 16, 19 and 24, Pascale Gueret 9, Photos.com 10, 15b, 22, 25b and 26, Hulton Archive/Stringer 17, Christophel Fine Art 21, fightbegin 28, Artistan 29t; Shutterstock: Everett Historical cover, 3b, 4, 13, 25t and 30, Morphart Creation 3t and 12, Paramonov Alexander 5, Bjoern Wylezich 15t, Roman Belogorodov 27, Anastasia Petrova 29b.
All design elements from Shutterstock.

All words in **bold** appear in the glossary on page 30.

CONTENTS

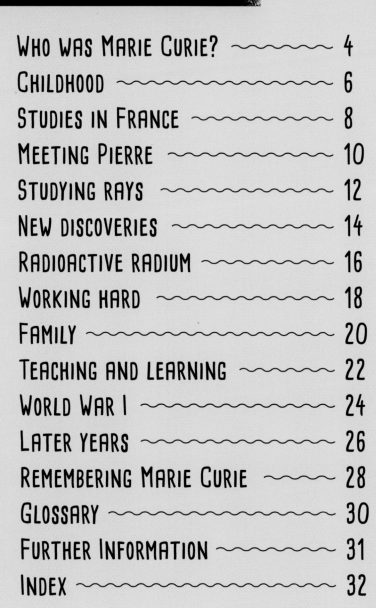

88
Ra

84
Po

WHO WAS MARIE CURIE?

Marie Curie was a Polish and French scientist. She was a **pioneering** physicist who studied radioactivity (see page 13), along with her husband, Pierre. Radioactivity had only just been discovered and the Curies' work was groundbreaking.

Marie Curie worked at a time when few women worked in science. Despite her great scientific achievements, many people did not take her seriously because she was a woman.

Marie Curie won the Nobel Prize twice. She won the Nobel Prize for Physics with Pierre in 1903, and then the Nobel Prize for Chemistry on her own in 1911.

She was the first woman to win a Nobel Prize and the first and only person ever to win Nobel Prizes for two different science subjects.

the Swedish scientist Alfred Nobel

the Nobel medal

NAT·
MDCCC
XXXIII
OB·
MDCCC
XCVI

ALFR·
NOBEL

The Nobel Prize is a very important prize for scientists who have made great discoveries, with winners such as Albert Einstein.

CHILDHOOD

Marie was born with the Polish name Maria Skłodowska on November 7, 1867 in Warsaw, Poland. Her father taught physics and math. He passed his love for science on to all of his children. Marie's mother was the headmistress of a girls' school.

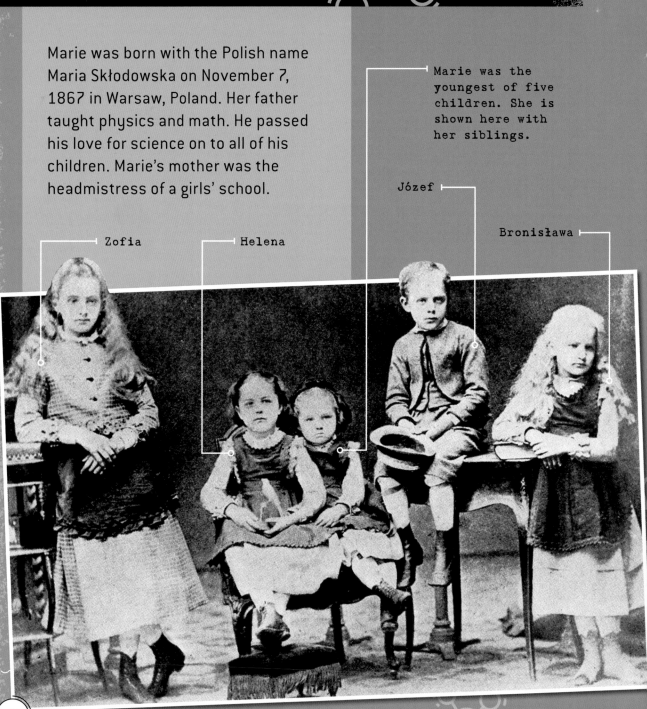

Marie was the youngest of five children. She is shown here with her siblings.

Zofia

Helena

Józef

Bronisława

Marie's childhood had sad and difficult moments. Her older sister Zofia died when Marie was seven, followed by their mother's death three years later.

Marie focused on her studies to help her cope. She wanted to go to college when she finished school, but women in Poland weren't allowed to at that time.

To continue her education, Marie went to secret science and history classes, which were known as the "Flying University."

The "Flying University" (see page 7) wasn't enough for Marie. She came up with a plan for her and her sister Bronisława to attend Sorbonne University in Paris, which was open to women. Marie would get a job to pay for Bronisława's tuition fees, and then Bronisława would do the same for her.

Marie paid for Bronisława's medical education in Paris by working as a **governess** in Poland.

Marie

Bronisława

In 1891, Marie moved to Paris. She started going to classes at the world-famous Sorbonne University. She was top of the class in her first **degree** in physical sciences (physics, chemistry, astronomy). She completed a degree in math a year later. After her degrees, she began to work in **research**.

At college, Marie was taught by some of the greatest scientists of the time.

Sorbonne University

Pierre taught
students at
the Sorbonne.

Pierre Curie was born on May 15, 1859 in Paris. He was educated by his father, who was a doctor. Pierre worked at the Sorbonne with his brother, Jacques, who was also a scientist. They did important research into crystals and magnets.

Pierre met Marie in 1894. They shared an interest in science and became closer when Marie started working in Pierre's **laboratory**. A year later, they got married and enjoyed a strong, happy relationship.

Pierre and Marie often took cycling trips in their free time.

STUDYING RAYS

In 1895, a scientist called Wilhelm Röntgen (1845–1923) discovered **X-rays** and made the first X-ray images. He realized that X-rays pass through soft materials, such as skin and muscle, but are blocked by hard materials, such as bones.

This is one of Röntgen's X-ray images. The X-rays pass through the flesh of the hand, but are blocked by bone and metal.

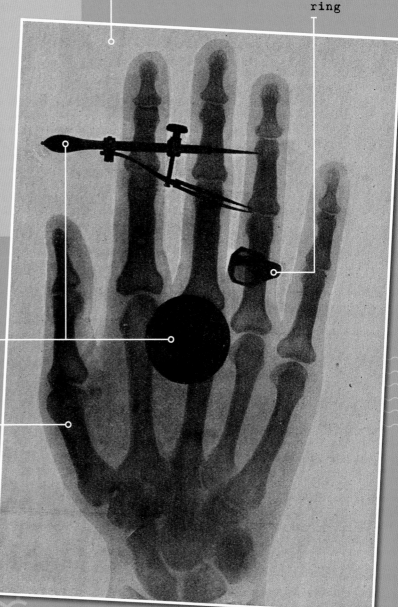

ring

metal scientific instruments

bone

Marie was very interested in X-rays. She started investigating the **element** uranium, which gave off rays similar to X-rays. Marie created the word "**radioactive**" to describe a material that gives off rays, such as uranium.

After testing uranium, Marie started testing other substances to see if they were radioactive. She found that a **compound** called pitchblende gave off more rays than uranium.

Marie and Pierre researched uranium and pitchblende together.

NEW DISCOVERIES

Marie thought that pitchblende probably contained radioactive elements that gave off rays. However, these elements had never been identified before. The Curies started working on **extracting** the mystery elements.

No one at the time knew of the dangers of **radiation** from radioactive elements. Radiation damages the cells in the body. Over a long period of time, high levels of radiation cause diseases, such as cancer.

Marie focused on how to extract the element, while Pierre studied the radiation it produced.

The work was very difficult. The pitchblende had to be ground into a powder, and then boiled and processed. Finally, they sent an electric current through it. In the spring of 1899, the Curies finally extracted one of the mystery radioactive elements. They named it polonium after Poland.

the chemical symbol for polonium

84
Po

Pitchblende is a blackish-gray rock. The Curies needed huge amounts of pitchblende for their experiments.

Laboratory workers helped to prepare pitchblende for the Curies' experiments.

pans of processing pitchblende

open coal fire

RADIOACTIVE RADIUM

After discovering polonium, Marie Curie realized that there was another radioactive element in pitchblende. The Curies worked for years to separate out the mystery element. It was hard work but they didn't give up.

Pierre invented a machine called an electrometer that measured the invisible rays produced by pitchblende.

88
Ra

the chemical symbol for radium

In 1902, the Curies finally extracted a tiny amount of the mystery element. They named the element radium.

The name "radium" is taken from the Latin word radius meaning ray. Although radium is a silvery metal, it emits powerful light rays that cause it to glow in the dark.

The Curies touched many radioactive substances, unaware of the danger.

glowing radium

The Curies won the Nobel Prize for their discovery of radium. Marie's name wasn't originally on the prize because she was a woman. However, it was added after Pierre complained.

The couple became famous. But they weren't interested in fame—they just wanted to carry on with their research.

The Curies' discovery made the headlines of many newspapers. This French newspaper shows the Curies in their laboratory.

As well as their research, the Curies had other jobs. Pierre continued teaching at Sorbonne University, while Marie worked as a **lecturer** in physics at a women's university. She also worked as an assistant in Pierre's laboratory.

Marie posed with some of her students from the women's university in 1904.

Pierre and Marie had two daughters. Irène was born in 1897, followed by Ève in 1904. Marie continued working. She hired nannies to take care of their daughters while she carried on with her research.

Marie taught her daughters to speak Polish, her first language. They also learned how to speak French.

Ève

Irène

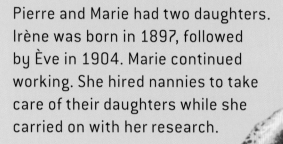

Sadly, the Curie family was torn apart when Pierre was killed in 1906. He died when he was hit by a horse and cart. Marie was heartbroken. She distracted herself by focusing on her research. She also took over Pierre's teaching position at the Sorbonne.

Marie was the first woman to teach at the Sorbonne. Many people came to her lectures.

demonstrating scientific equipment

Marie continued with the couple's work after Pierre's death. In 1911, she won her second Nobel Prize. She started work at a new laboratory that only focused on research into radium. It was called the Radium Institute.

Marie Curie was in charge of the Radium Institute.

Alongside her research, Marie gave science classes to her daughters and the children of her friends, most of whom were around 10 years old. Other parents taught the children different subjects, such as history and German. They wanted the children to learn from experts, not just from school.

Irène went on to study science and work alongside Marie as her assistant. She won her own Nobel Prize in 1935 alongside her husband Frédéric Joliot-Curie.

WORLD WAR I

In the summer of 1914, World War I broke out in Europe. There was lots of fighting in France. By bringing X-ray machines close to the battlefields, Marie played an important role in treating injured soldiers. The machines were used to identify the soldiers' injuries.

Marie and her daughter Irène helped to train doctors and nurses to use the X-ray equipment.

Many soldiers were badly injured during fighting.

It was hard to get X-ray machines to some locations. So Marie developed a **mobile** X-ray unit that fit inside vans. The vans could be driven wherever they were needed.

Marie is seen here behind the wheel of one of her X-ray vans, which were known as Little Curies.

After World War I ended in 1918, Marie traveled as a guest of honor, giving lectures around the world. She also helped to set up research centers in Paris and Poland. In these centers, scientists continued the Curies' research.

Marie met US President Warren G. Harding on a trip to the USA in 1921.

No one was aware of the dangers of radiation while the Curies were carrying out their radioactivity research. They didn't take any safety measures and Marie was exposed to a huge amount of radiation. This led to her developing **leukemia** (blood cancer). She died of it on July 4, 1934 at the age of 66.

Marie's tomb

Pierre's tomb

The tombs of Pierre and Marie Curie lie in the Panthéon, Paris. Many important French people have been laid to rest here, including Marie, who had become a French citizen.

REMEMBERING MARIE CURIE

Marie Curie is remembered around the world for her pioneering research and amazing discoveries. She is also celebrated for being a trailblazing woman in science at a time when women did not have the same opportunities or recognition as men.

a model of a polonium atom

A statue dedicated to Marie Curie stands in her birthplace of Warsaw, Poland. There are many other statues of her around the world.

Marie Curie's Polish name

MARIA SKŁODOWSKA-CURIE

Marie's research has had a huge impact on medicine. Today, doctors know how to use radiation safely to treat and cure cancer. Research continues at the Radium Institute to develop new, safe uses for radiation.

In the UK, a charity to help people with cancer has been named after Marie Curie.

This mural celebrating Marie's achievements is painted on the house in which she was born in Warsaw. The mural includes the symbols for polonium and radium.

GLOSSARY

compound: A substance made up of two or more elements

degree: A qualification you receive after finishing a college course

element: A substance that can't be broken down into any other substance

extract: To take something out

governess: A woman whose job it is to teach children in their home

laboratory: A room used for scientific work, such as research and experiments

lecturer: Someone who teaches at a university

leukemia: Blood cancer (a serious disease)

mobile: Describes something that can be moved easily

pioneering: Starting the development of something important

radiation: Energy in the form of invisible rays

radioactive: Describes something that gives off rays (radiation)

research: Studying something in order to get more information about it

X-ray: A type of energy ray

TIMELINE

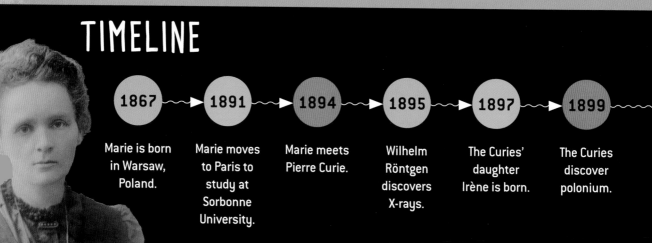

1867
Marie is born in Warsaw, Poland.

1891
Marie moves to Paris to study at Sorbonne University.

1894
Marie meets Pierre Curie.

1895
Wilhelm Röntgen discovers X-rays.

1897
The Curies' daughter Irène is born.

1899
The Curies discover polonium.

FURTHER INFORMATION

BOOKS

Who Was Marie Curie?
by Megan Stine
(Penguin Workshop, 2014)

Marie Curie and the Power of Persistence
by Karla Valenti
(Sourcebooks, 2020)

Women in Science
by Rachel Ignotofsky
(Ten Speed Press, 2016)

WEBSITES

www.britannica.com/biography/Marie-Curie
Read more about the biography of Marie Curie

www.youtube.com/watch?v=aowghaUvP6Q
Watch a video about the amazing life of Marie Curie

www.mariecurie.org.uk/who/our-history/marie-curie-the-scientist
Learn more about the charity named after Marie Curie, and why they chose to honor her in this way

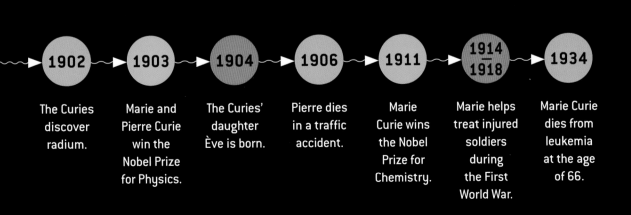

1902	1903	1904	1906	1911	1914–1918	1934
The Curies discover radium.	Marie and Pierre Curie win the Nobel Prize for Physics.	The Curies' daughter Ève is born.	Pierre dies in a traffic accident.	Marie Curie wins the Nobel Prize for Chemistry.	Marie helps treat injured soldiers during the First World War.	Marie Curie dies from leukemia at the age of 66.

INDEX

More titles in the **Masterminds** series

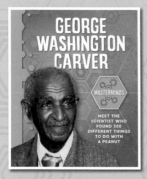

Who was George Washington Carver?
Childhood
Freedom
Getting an education
Farm studies
New crops
Peanut products
The sweet potato
Making a change
Colourful dyes
Honours
Later life
Remembering Carver

Who was Marie Curie?
Childhood
Studies in France
Meeting Pierre
Studying rays
New discoveries
Radioactive radium
Working hard
Family
Teaching and learning
The First World War
Later years
Remembering Marie Curie

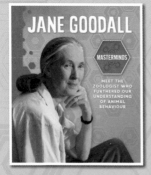

Who is Jane Goodall?
Childhood
Off to Africa
Ancestors and evolution
Living with chimpanzees
New discoveries
Back to school
Family
Inspiring others
Books
The Jane Goodall Institute
Activism
Celebrating Jane Goodall

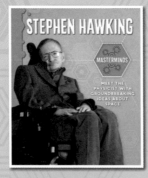

Who was Stephen Hawking?
Childhood
University days
Family
Space-time study
Black holes
A new voice
Sharing science
The future
Adventures
The Theory of Everything
Awards
Remembering Stephen Hawking

Who is Katherine Johnson?
Bright beginnings
Getting ahead
Teaching and family
A new job
Fighting prejudice
Into space
In orbit
To the Moon
Later life
Hidden Figures
Celebrating Katherine Johnson
A new generation

Who was Nikola Tesla?
Childhood
University studies
Bright ideas
Off to the USA
Tesla vs Edison
In the laboratory
Lighting the world
Free energy
Awards and honours
Later life
Remembering Tesla
Legacy

Also available: Rosalind Franklin, Leonardo da Vinci